CUCKOO

by Lisa Carroll

SAMUEL FRENCH

samuelfrench.co.uk

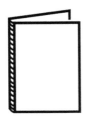

MUSIC USE NOTE

Licensees are solely responsible for obtaining formal written permission from copyright owners to use copyrighted music in the performance of this play and are strongly cautioned to do so. If no such permission is obtained by the licensee, then the licensee must use only original music that the licensee owns and controls. Licensees are solely responsible and liable for all music clearances and shall indemnify the copyright owners of the play(s) and their licensing agent, Samuel French, against any costs, expenses, losses and liabilities arising from the use of music by licensees. Please contact the appropriate music licensing authority in your territory for the rights to any incidental music.

USE OF COPYRIGHT MUSIC

A licence issued by Samuel French Ltd to perform this play does not include permission to use the incidental music specified in this copy.

Where the place of performance is already licensed by the PERFORMING RIGHT SOCIETY (PRS) a return of the music used must be made to them. If the place of performance is not so licensed then application should be made to the PRS, 2 Pancras Square, London, N1C 4AG.

A separate and additional licence from PHONOGRAPHIC PERFORMANCE LTD, 1 Upper James Street, London W1F 9DE (www.ppluk.com) is needed whenever commercial recordings are used.

IMPORTANT BILLING AND CREDIT REQUIREMENTS

If you have obtained performance rights to this title, please refer to your licensing agreement for important billing and credit requirements.

ABOUT THE AUTHOR

Lisa is an Irish playwright based in London. Lisa trained on the Foundation Course at RADA and graduated from University College Dublin in 2012 with a BA in English. She has undertaken writing programmes at the Lyric Hammersmith, the Royal Court and Headlong. *Cuckoo* is Lisa's debut full-length play, and was shortlisted for the Papatango Prize and Verity Bargate award. Previous work includes: *Three Cities* (Edinburgh Fringe), *Poultry* (Miniaturists), *Catcall* (RADA), *Róisín* (Old Red Lion), and *Snapdragon* (Abbey Theatre).

Photo © Ste Murray

AUTHOR'S NOTE

SETTING

The play is set in Crumlin, Dublin 12, today. The action is chronological.

CASTING

The cast should reflect the diversity of its audience and the world around us.

PINGU

It is crucial that the actor playing Pingu identifies as non-binary and/or genderqueer. Pingu expresses themselves non-verbally, though this is never caricatured, signed or mimed. They are not mute, they have chosen not to speak.

PUNCTUATION AND STAGE DIRECTIONS

A slash (/) indicates where one character begins speaking over another

A dash (–) indicates that the character speaking is cut off by an interruption from another character, or a thought cutting across

Ellipses (...) suggest space for thought in the line, or in PINGU's case, a thought or response.

A space within a character's lines suggests a pause, hesitation, thought, and/or change in tactics. These need to be acknowledged in performance.

A (beat.) is shorter than a (pause.) which is shorter than a (silence.)

Codas indicate moments of visual storytelling which advance plot and/or reveal character.

WITH THANKS TO

Everyone at Samuel French. Debbie Hannan, George Warren, Mary Nighy, Nick Quinn, Maeve Bolger, Chris Truscott, Deirdre O'Halloran, Jess Traynor, Ruth McGowan, Emilie Pine, Stewart Pringle, Sam Potter, Sarah Madigan, Ciarán Owens, Milly Thomas, Ste, Foxy, Seb, Kit, Oli and Al – thank you.

Caitríona, Elise, Sade, Colin, Peter, Jess, Basia (oh my God I know), Dom, Mel, Sofi and Andre – thank you.

My brilliant and supportive colleagues, especially Laura.

Erin Cressida Wilson – you started this.

The Squids. Dobby. My Mum and Dad.

Thank you.

For my family and friends.

Cuckoo was first presented by Metal Rabbit Productions at
Soho Theatre, on 13 November 2018 with the following cast
and creatives:

IONA	Caitríona Ennis
PINGU	Elise Heaven
POCKETS	Colin Campbell
TOLLER	Sade Malone
TRIX	Peter Newington

Directed by	Debbie Hannan
Produced by	Sofi Berenger &
	George Warren
Designed by	Basia Bińkowska
Lighting Design by	Jessica Hung Han Yun
Sound Design by	Dominic Brennan

CHARACTERS

IONA – female, 16 years old, Irish
PINGU – non-binary, 16 years old, Irish
TRIX – male, 17 years old, Irish
POCKETS – male, 17 years old, Irish
TOLLER – female, 16 years old, Irish

ACT ONE

Overture

*Conor McGregor's sister's voicemail to the dog groomers, mixed with "**DIAMONDS**" by Rihanna.*

---

* A licence to produce CUCKOO does not include a performance licence for "DIAMONDS". For further information, please see Music Use Note on page v.

Scene One
Thank Fuck For Ryanair

Crumlin. The Old County Glen Estate. Friday Night.

Down the back of IONA'*s high-walled back garden. The house is dark and empty.*

We can hear the distant sound of thudding bass from a party we're not invited to. It reverberates around the garden and, each time it peaks, only intensifies IONA'*s misery.*

IONA *(16) was born with all the intensity of a speeding freight-train, and to this day she's never been able to slow down. Entirely un-self-conscious and yet utterly self-conscious, people don't know what to do with her as much as she doesn't know what to do with herself. N.B* IONA *is pronounced "eye-own-ah".*

Her dress style is an attempt at cool, but she just doesn't have the eye to hit the mark, her own eclectic tastes breaking out despite her best efforts. Her footwear right now is the exception – there's no world in which these are cool and even IONA *knows it – she's in a huge, ungainly pair of white Crocs and they are awful. Plus, today she has egg dried into her hair and jumper. She's in a stinking mood.*

PINGU *(16) has gone by this name since the age of 12, and is known for their signature tailcoat – a penguin in name and appearance.* PINGU *identifies as non-binary, uses they/them pronouns, and presents as androgynous – which is to say it's tricky to decipher whether* PINGU *is 'male' or 'female' by their outward appearance, and this is very much deliberate.* PINGU *does not present as either gender, but something else entirely.*

PINGU *does not speak – but is absolutely not mute.* PINGU *knows exactly how and when to use silence (and speech, should they choose) and, despite quite some level of inner turmoil, outwardly comes off as calm and confident thanks to an unflinching and piercing thousand-yard stare.*

PINGU *communicates subtly and non-verbally, using silence, eye contact, or choosing not to communicate. It is never pantomimic or charades,* IONA *and* PINGU *have been friends for such a long time – they are close to the point of being symbiotic – that often, not always, but often,* IONA *knows full well what* PINGU *means: words aren't necessary. However, often around people they are not comfortable with,* PINGU *wears a poker face which is indecipherable.*

Today, PINGU*'s tailcoat is splattered in a congealing murky liquid.*

IONA – ya have ta give the fellas doin' it on the regs some credit like cos it's not fuckin' easy – at least two days in preparation – like mental preparation as well as logistical like: gettin' there, actin' cool calm and collected, escape routes and tha' – as well as a good half day the day itself, between gettin' down to Blackrock –

PINGU ...

IONA Well the way I thought was tha' if you go somewhere everyone's rollin' in ih, they're not gonna expect people ta be swipin' stuff since everyone can afford it annyway

PINGU ...

IONA Wha'? Eh, NO that is a flawless logic

PINGU ...

IONA Am I tellin' this story?

PINGU ...

IONA Yeh so I sit my little ass on the seventeen down to Blackrock shopping centre – happy out. Gonna get meself a handy pair'a them Rihanna Pumas – it's the Creepers I've me eye on, but I'm not gonna say no to them furry sliders either –

A burst of distant music and a roar of laughter. This catches IONA. *She listens longingly, her heart sinking.*

Cos I'm thinkin' – there is no way – no WAY Toller can deny the power of Rihanna – there's no WAY I won't get in ta Pocket's 17th birthday wearin' them Creepers

So I get there, righ' – my gut's goin' mad, I'm absolutely shittin' it, but I'm just about managin' to control me shakes. So to start, I'm doing some casual light browsing, set the groundwork righ', you know, for the cameras and security and tha': that I'm just here lightly touching the goods on display, ya know, I'm a regular Joe who totally belongs here

PINGU ...

IONA What!!?? Yeh, lightly touching! You know, pick it up, inspect it, put it back down! Wouldn't be doing that if I was there to swipe it would I, I'd not be puttin' it back, would I? GENIUS.

PINGU ...

IONA So finally righ', I've done me recce, I've curated an image of *indescribable* wealth – and now it's time ta pally up to the attendant, try them on – cos God Forbid I'd go to all that trouble ta nick a pair that didn't bleedin' fit, d'ya know?

PINGU ...

IONA So I've got them, they're fittin' nice and snug an' I'm lookin' *real* well, and the attendant's hovering – all eyes and teeth: "Can I get anything else for ya there pet?" – "No thanks," says I – "just need ta have a think about these, I'm not *totally* convinced," and after a bit of tramping up and down and humming and hawing she finally fucks off into the back to get me another size – THAT I DON'T NEED WHAAAAAAAAA'!?

Now it's time to stall ih, I've left her me aul piece'a shit runners in the box – don't need them anymore thank you – and I'm swannin' outa there like I fuckin' own the place in me new kicks – CHEERS Robin Fenty more commonly known as multi-platinum selling artist, Rihanna.

Then, there I am, a good five if not six paces out the door when I feel – you guessed ih – the dreaded hand on the aul shoulder. Huge fucker, looks like he eats children for breakfast,

"Here, let's see what's in that bag of yours missy"

Well.

"Be my fuckin' guest sugartits," I tell him and I open that baby up wide: "have a good rummage."

And this is the bit that *really* fuckin' pissed me off – he looks at me when I says that and kinda snorts at me an' says, "You're a bit of a handful aren't ya?"

You know what Pingu?

I swear. Someone comes to me all "You're too much Iona" ... "You're a handful Iona" ... "Tone it down Iona" ...EVER again – I'll take their fucking eyes out with me fingernails. I'll slice them from crown to fucking chin. I'll go cata-fuckin'-tonic is what I'll do. It'll be like a nuclear explosion down in Crumlin. People'll think the IRA're back. People'll think someone's finally taken out The Monk and it's out an' out warfare. I'll fucking...

PINGU ...

IONA Sorry –

Yeh – ehhhhhhh – yeh, now I've just seen your one the shop assistant reappear from the back so I've not got time to rip him a new arsehole – so I simply tell him that between being bald, ugly and overweigh', he looks like a giant thumb, and then I'm away on the bus, victorious, fuckin' buzzin' I am.

PINGU ...

IONA Yeh well relax the kaks cos it was a sharp downhill from there babes – amen't I on the 17 home all thrilled wit' meself – *well* on time to meet you – an' I can *tell* today's finally our fuckin' day!

Don't I get off on Bangor Road – the *moment* me two feet hit the kerb, who clocks me?

Kelly Phelan an' her mangy crew of harpies.

It's like one'a them slow-mo moments in the movies...she looks at me... I look at her...an' I do me best ta' silently communicate: 'No bitch...not taday, not ta-fuckin'-day' – but sure she's not half as telepathic as you Pingu cos next thing aren't they peggin' it towards me full speed? I'm only little now I'm no Mo Farah but I manage ta pelt it down towards the football club an' eventually they give up. Next thing don't I realise me phone's fallen outta me pocket an' all so I can't even text ya?

So I'm guessin' this is when –

PINGU ...

IONA *picks at some of the smoothie on* PINGU*'s coat.*

IONA Fuckin' cunts

Get ta Pocket's house fit ta collapse, but still...still holdin' out a hope in the power of this footwear gold – plus at this point I'm thinkin' you must've got in cos there's no sign of ya – so I'm feelin pretty *bold*

...

I swear to God there's a special place reserved in hell for Toller.

PINGU *nods. Cunt.*

Toller opens the door face on her like a bag a' spiders

"I was wonderin' when you'd try your luck," she says. "Your little mate was just here."

Honestly it felt like I'd swallowed a rock hearin' tha'

"You'd wanna tell that weirdo they'd have a much better chance a' gettin' in if they'd ditch that FUCKIN' AWFUL SUIT"

Then she looks at my feet

I'm thinkin'

Maybe this is the moment's gonna change everything

She'll take it back

Apologise

Tell me she didn't realise I was such a fashionable legend

"Girls!" she roars – next thing, Kelly has me in a headlock, Sharon's me left arm and Fiona my right, cos I'm scratching like a motherfucker, and there's Tara and Clare ripping them off me feet, and there's me squirming like a fuckin' centipede while Toller just stands there watchin'

I was the proud owner of them Creepers for an hour, Pingu.

An HOUR.

"When're you gonna get it inta your head that it is *never* gonna happen Iona?"

That's when I notice she's holdin' a box of eggs an' all

For an actual second I was thinkin' to meself well eggs aren't really a very good party snack so that's weird

Then I realise...

Eggs actually hurt quite a lot when they smash in your face like these were like quite sturdy eggs

Phelan flings my phone at me, they're laughing at me like a pack a'hyenas while I stand there drippin', everyone recordin' me.

Then Toller comes righ' up in my face, bout four inches of makeup on her:

"You an' your little pal come here again, we'll have your eyes out of their sockets alrigh'? Now *fuck* off."

They sit in their shared misery for a moment.

*A back door opens and with it, a burst of music floods
the estate once more,* IONA *wilts.*

Fuckin' sick'a this place.

A pause for as long as it takes.

I just *wish* they'd –

But PINGU *jumps up, giving the finger towards the party.
They are done. Maybe they chuck something towards
the revellers.*

IONA *sits in misery. Suddenly they pull their phone
out, open the Ryanair app and show* IONA *the screen.*

Ah Pingu...

PINGU ...

IONA I've *told* ya –

PINGU ...

IONA You've never even been ta London you've no *idea* what
it's like

PINGU ...

IONA ...you're talking about moving *country* here I mean...

Where'd we stay?

PINGU ...

IONA Mam won't tell me where he lives

I mean he's probably in one of the real swanky bits,
Kensington or... Croydon or somethin', but...

She gets real weird when I ask her

...I'm dyin' ta see him

PINGU ...

IONA *gets up, paces.*

IONA Ach... I dunno...

What about money? ...what about...

IONA *quickly realises she's in great discomfort.*

...what tha' fuck

...what tha' fuck is this...???

She reaches down her pants...it's a load of egg.

I'VE GOT EGG ALL OVER MY ARSE

AGHHHHHHHHHHHHHHHHHHHHHHHHHHHHHHH
HHHHHHHHHHHHHHHHHH

She starts lobbing egg remnants towards the party.

YOU FUCKERS!!!!! YOU ABSOLUTE FUCKERS!!!! THAT IS SO UNPLEASANT!

Fuck it Pingu we're goin'. We're goin'.

PINGU ...

IONA I'm serious Pingu we're outta here – fuck this

PINGU ...!!!

IONA We're fuckin' doin' it – thank fuck for Ryanair, ha?

PINGU ...

IONA We're gonna smash it over there. We are gonna be fuckin' swanning around London like we own the fuckin' place. You know wha' – we don't need Toller an' them – we're gonna be friends with... Ri-fuckin'-Anna – that's who we'll be hangin' with – I'll have Creepers comin' out my fuckin' ears!

They dance, they celebrate, the relief on **PINGU** *is palpable.*

IONA *stops and looks at* **PINGU**.

Pingu?

PINGU ...

IONA Would ya think about talkin' again when we get there?

PINGU *stops and thinks.*

It's a good question.

Scene Two
Rumble In Tha Crumble

We're in POCKETS' *back garden. Daybreak. It's the tail end of the party* IONA *so desperately wanted in on. Just about everyone is gone. Music still thuds lightly from the house. The garden is strewn with cans and debris.*

POCKETS *(17) is a fellow of more brawn than brain, but a man whose reputation does most of the hard work for him.*

TRIX *(16) is a young man of quick mind who at least believes he has more charm than he knows what to do with. He holds his paws up for* POCKETS, *who is practising combos.*

TRIX Jesus they should be calling you The Notorious, wha'!!?

POCKETS I'd make shit of Conor McGregor

TRIX Oh yeah I'd say ya would

POCKETS I would!

TRIX I know ya would!

POCKETS I fuckin' would!

TRIX I believe ya!

POCKETS I would!

TRIX You would, I know, you would!

Pause. A stand off. POCKETS *eyes* TRIX.

POCKETS I was in his car

TRIX You were in his car?

POCKETS In his green Lamborghini yeh

TRIX You were in a Lamborghini!?

POCKETS I was, I was in Conor McGregor's Lamborghini

TRIX You were in Conor McGregor's green Lamborghini?

POCKETS You a parrot or somethin'?

Beat.

TRIX When was tha'?

POCKETS That time he came back ta Crumlin before Mayweather

TRIX And you were in his car!?

POCKETS Didn't I just tell ya!?

They are interrupted by **TOLLER** *(16) worse for wear but still looking well and high on life. She is brash as they come and can deliver an insult that'd slice you up down and sideways. She's got a pretty swank pair of new runners on. Maroon. Velvet. Pumas.*

N.B **TOLLER** *is pronounced like dollar.*

TOLLER HOWIYEEEEEEEEEE! ANOTHER RUMBLE IN THE FUCKIN' CRUMBLE DOWN! LAST NIGHT WAS UN-FUCKIN-REAL LADS! YOU KNOW WHAT I SAY? FUCK ANYONE WHO TELLS YA CRUMLIN'S NOT WHERE IT'S FUCKIN' AT? YOU KNOW WHAT I HAVE? LUCOZADE!

TOLLER *tosses a bottle each to* **POCKETS** *and* **TRIX**.

Get that inta ya –

ALL – YA SLUT YA!

They all drink and come up for air at the same time.

POCKETS Unrale

TRIX I don't know what they put in it

TOLLER It's like crack

They all drink again. Then finish, gasp, and chuck their bottles away.

TRIX Here was Pockets ever in McGregor's green Lamborghini?

TOLLER Pffffff –

But POCKETS *shoots her a look.*

Ah he was yeh. Good few times.

POCKETS It's got a flame thrower an' all.

POCKETS *motions for* TRIX *to put his hands up.*

TOLLER Here lads – I've GOT to show you this video, I was fuckin' dyin' –

TRIX Here d'ya know who thinks he's a real Billy big bollocks? That Conor Guilfoyle –

TOLLER Lads –

POCKETS Ah he's a gobshite

TOLLER I told Kelly Phelan to put a chilli in her eye – as a joke like – and she fuckin' did ih! Honestly, you'll be dyin' –

TOLLER *pats herself down. Her glee soon turns to horror.*

Where's my phone? Where's my fuckin' iPhone?

TOLLER *bolts back into the house.*

As soon as he's sure she's gone, TRIX *takes* TOLLER*'s phone out of his back pocket – it's clearly hers, the case is pink and glittery – flashes it at* POCKETS *along with a wink, and replaces it.*

TRIX Burstin' with dickpicks

POCKETS Ah jaysus that's my cousin man

They box.

TRIX Did I hear Guilfoyle said somethin' bout your Da – did I hear that righ'?

POCKETS What'd he say?

TOLLER *re-enters in a blind panic.*

TOLLER I can't find the fuckin' thing anywhere lads Mam'll have me fuckin' head on a plate over this –

POCKETS Where's he live again?

TOLLER LADS! ME PHONE

TRIX Up by the KCR I think

TOLLER It's pink and it's got this furry bit?

TRIX Not seen it

Unseen by **TOLLER**, **TRIX** *has lobbed her phone a few feet away. But to* **TOLLER**, *all hope is gone.*

TOLLER Ah fuck lads

I'm a dead woman

LADS!?

TRIX *points glibly over to where he threw the phone.*

TRIX What's tha'?

TOLLER Hah?

TOLLER *leaps up, rushes over, grabs the phone and – once her relief has passed – she turns on* **TRIX**.

You're a little SCROT ya know tha'?

She goes for **TRIX**, *trying to slap him, but he's far too quick for her. He cackles – this is the best part of the game.*

TRIX I didn't do anythin'? Pockets, did you see me doin' anything?

TOLLER You KNOW how precious that device is to me!!!

TRIX You should take better care of it then shouldn't ya!?

TOLLER *(to* **POCKETS***)* You're an enabler an' all –

POCKETS Toller get this place cleaned up

TOLLER Ah gimme a minute wouldja not even looked at me Insta yet today

TOLLER *sits down and starts scrolling.*

POCKETS Toller!

TOLLER I said in a minute!

POCKETS *waits.* **TOLLER** *gets up.* **POCKETS** *hands her the bin bag and she starts collecting cans.*

TRIX Here any birds last nigh'?

POCKETS Nah nothin' special

TRIX *(full of himself)* Do you know Clare Doyle?

TOLLER ...Here – lads –

POCKETS Yeh. Shifted her at Toner's birthday last year

TRIX ...Oh

TOLLER Lads!

POCKETS Better up your game mate

TOLLER LISTEN WOULDJA?

POCKETS WHAT?

TOLLER You know your one Iona?

POCKETS ...Who?

TOLLER Hangs round with your one Pingu, real weird fucker

POCKETS *Pingu*? Kinda name's tha'?

TOLLER She lives at number 14 – Iona – tried ta get in here last nigh' but I sent her packin'

TRIX What about her?

TOLLER They're goin' ta London!?

POCKETS ...So what they're goin' on their holliers?

TOLLER No no no *goin'* goin – leavin' like. For good.

Beat.

POCKETS What's wrong with Crumlin?

TOLLER Good fuckin' riddance –

TRIX When're they goin'?

TOLLER That girl's me driven demented for *years* –

TRIX Toller *when* are they goin'?

TOLLER ...tomorrow it says

Beat.

TRIX 24 hours

POCKETS No chance.

Nah, *no* chance.

TOLLER *looks up at the two boys, from one to the other like she's at a tennis match.*

TOLLER What? ...

What!?

Scene Three
Don't Know What Ya Got Til It's Gone

Texas Fried Chicken, Crumlin shopping centre.

PINGU *is avidly concentrating on their phone,* IONA *returns to the table with two fresh snackboxes and plonks them down.* PINGU *pushes the snackbox away, indicating the phone.*

IONA Ah you're not full. I'm fuckin' starvin' – emigrating's giving me a serious hunger. You'll be grand, two snackboxes you'll be fine, three now you'd be shittin' your pants all the way to the airport.

PINGU *focuses on the phone,* IONA *lashes into a chicken thigh.*

I'll not miss a lot about this place but I'll miss Texas Fried Chicken with all me heart.

What if the chicken in London's sub par?

PINGU ...

IONA Here none of this early morning cheap flight carry on – fucked if I'm getting up at the crack'a dawn

PINGU ...

IONA Well make sure you book the speedy boarding stuff, priority and all tha' – don't be scrimpin' on me

PINGU *puts the phone down and looks at* IONA.

Okay I trust you. You book whatever. Just make sure we're not in shit seats. Like at the back. Or middle seats. Or near crying babies. Aisle or window's fine.

PINGU *chuckles.*

Ah there we go! You love ih! You'll be stuck with me now

They smile at one another, IONA *gorges on her food.* PINGU *takes a handful of chips and gets back to booking.*

The boys swagger in.

TRIX Ah there she is!!! Jesus Iona you are a vision today

PINGU *leaps up, pulling* **IONA** *up, on high alert.*

IONA Jesus look I'm sorry lads I shouldn'ta just turned up at the door like tha' I just thought ye might let me in for /a while like –

POCKETS Woah woah woah – what're ya talkin' about?

IONA Look tell Toller I'm sorry an' here – we'll leave – here – take our table whydoncha – there's a snackbox there if ya want it – fresh like, barely touched –

PINGU *edges towards the door.*

TRIX Iona?

IONA Eh... Yeh?

TRIX Are ya well?

IONA Eh. Yeh yeh I'm / alr –

TRIX Cos you're lookin' well

IONA *and* **PINGU** *exchange looks. Um...what?*

IONA Eh. Cheers Trix

You also...look well.

POCKETS Yeah you're lookin' very well Iona, very well, I was sayin' that ta Trix before actually, you're a great lookin' girl

TRIX You were sayin' that ta me before?

POCKETS *(to* **IONA***)* I was.

(to **TRIX***)* I fuckin' was.

IONA Ehm. Thanks lads. Here we'll be seein' ya –

TRIX Can I get ya some chicken?

IONA Eh –

POCKETS No here I'll get ya some chicken – snackbox?

TRIX I'll get the chicken, I'll get the chicken – you deserve no less than a family bucket – not some piddly snackbox jaysus

POCKETS Ah ya don't want a bucket ya want ta be mindin' that amazin figure'a yours – I'll get ya a snackbox – few goujons now

TRIX Are you serious I said I'm gettin' it

POCKETS Chicken for the lady, wha'?

> **TRIX** *isn't quite quick enough as* **POCKETS** *rushes to the counter.*

TRIX Sit down! Sit down!

> **TRIX** *almost pushes* **PINGU** *out of the way to sit next to* **IONA**. **PINGU** *is not impressed.*

Ehhh so here I hear the two'a you're movin'

IONA Eh yeh we're just bookin' the flights actually mad excited aren't we?

TRIX Fair play – how come youse're goin'?

IONA Oh eh...it's eh... The the socio-economic conditions.

Untenable, ya know?

TRIX Ah right yeh yeh I getcha same thing been gettin' me down lately as well yeh

IONA Really? Yeh cos while actually Ireland politically is now – at least on paper – an incredibly progressive country – we've a long way ta go – plus economically it's still the pits yeh – I mean this housin' crisis an' all, so just thought it was time ta take the plunge, ya know

Beat.

TRIX You've a real smart head on your shoulders, haven't ya?

IONA Eh...

TRIX So you were lookin' ta come to the party last nigh' was ih?

IONA Look –

TRIX Here pet we're not annoyed alrigh'?

IONA Yeh eh we only called round like, see what the story was, but then eh, decided ta leave it, ya know, not our scene, prefer the quiet life, we do, don't we?

TRIX Yeah I hear London's quiet enough

Anyway as I say...you're lookin' very well

As if only finally noticing them now:

Y'alrigh' ...Pingu is ih?

Beat. **PINGU** *gives* **TRIX** *nothing.*

Is it Pingu isn't ih?

Again, **PINGU** *is impervious.* **TRIX** *is rattled.*

POCKETS *rushes back over, his arms full – a bucket of chicken, chips, cans.*

POCKETS Here we are! Get that inta ya Cynthia!

POCKETS *shoves the bucket of chicken under* **IONA**'s *nose.*

I've not been feeling well today so I've not. When we heard the news – weren't we? We were devastated

TRIX Oh yeh absolutely devo yeh

POCKETS Sick to our stomachs

TRIX *Can't* believe you're leavin'

IONA Really?

TRIX She says it's the socio-economic conditions driven her out, that righ'?

IONA Yeh untenable

POCKETS Oh right yeh right...yeah bad craic the...yeh seriously bad craic that stuff. But anyway – heartbroken I am

IONA Ah thanks

We're lookin' forward to it aren't we?

PINGU *though is giving these two lads nothing.*

Pingu's over the bleedin' moon.

POCKETS Here where'll you live in London?

IONA Me Da's he's been in London these last few years livin' it up – he's mad successful – really big deal yeh

POCKETS Is he?

IONA Yeh yeh – yeh actually he's like really smashin' ih, he's over there ehm...he's a music producer.

TRIX No fuckin' way, really?

IONA Oh yeh! He's basically Pharrell but like. Irish. And Caucasian. An' he's only known in the UK. Massive though

PINGU *takes a slow, dissatisfied bite of chicken. Guess we're in for the long haul now.*

TRIX You're an impressive girl Iona, ya know tha'?

POCKETS She is – you are Iona – you're somethin' else

IONA Ehm

Wow, cheers

No one's ever said that ta me before

POCKETS Yeh definitely – yeh listen we were talkin' weren't we? And we were sayin' – you're such a great girl and we just didn't make the most of ya while you were here – it only really hits ya when someone's slipped through your fingers, ya know?

TRIX Yeh I was sayin' that ya just don't know what ya got til it's gone, that righ'?

POCKETS Yeh no it was me sayin' tha' – I was sayin' tha'

TRIX I said it

POCKETS So here we'll have ta hang out before ya head

IONA Sorry wha?

TRIX OH yeh – soak ya up, ya know, make the most of ya before ya leave

IONA Hang out...wit' you...?

POCKETS Course – here come over later

TRIX Nah come ta mine – I've a huge telly

POCKETS Don't bother it's tiny

TRIX It's not its massive it takes up the whole fuckin' wall

POCKETS Picture's shite

TRIX The pictures crystal clear it's literally like you're there – in the telly – it's outta this world

POCKETS Grainy, ya know, sound quality's bad too

TRIX Honestly you've never seen anything like ih you'll be transported

POCKETS Trix your house is a shithole

Beat.

TRIX ...it's not...

Beat.

PINGU *nudges* **IONA.**

IONA Sounds class lads, really does, but we need ta –

TRIX A party.

That's what you need – huge goin' away party –

POCKETS Oh God yeh – bleedin' massive

IONA REALLY!?

TRIX Yeh –

POCKETS OH jesus yeh – one for the ages.

IONA Oh my God!

POCKETS Yeh we'll have a righ' aul rager – really send ya off in style – sound good?

IONA DOES THE POPE SHIT IN THE WOODS!? YEAH!!!

PINGU slams their hands on the table – oh come on.

TRIX Sure you're invited Pingu

Beat.

POCKETS Yeh

Course –

TRIX Ah man I bet you two are the life an' soul – am I righ'?

IONA I mean we are yeh but –

POCKETS Iona this will be the gaffer of your wildest dreams – cans as far as the eye can see! You'll be my guests of honour.

IONA looks at PINGU, but PINGU's trying to get IONA outta there.

Here – why dontcha come over ta mine later – so we can plan it? *Anything* ya want.

Coda:

TOLLER's *room.*

TOLLER does her make-up impeccably.

The process is detailed and absorbing.

Content with her looks, takes a series of photos.

She films herself doing a dance routine to Rihanna's **"BITCH BETTER HAVE MY MONEY"***.

---

* A licence to produce *CUCKOO* does not include a performance licence for "BITCH BETTER HAVE MY MONEY". For further information, please see Music Use Note on page v.

Scene Four
Ya Can't Polish A Turd

IONA *stands over* TOLLER *as she does her makeup.*
TOLLER *catches sight of her in the mirror.*

TOLLER WHAT THA FUCK!?

IONA Howiya what's the craic – you're lookin' well – that an eyebrow tutorial is ih? Yeh I'm forever doin' them as well –

TOLLER How tha fuck did you get in my house!?

IONA Tommy let me in – he's gotten big hasn't he?

TOLLER TOMMY! – TOMMYYYYYYYY!

IONA I think he went out playin' – so! Wow this place has changed, went mad with the pink didn't ya?

TOLLER What the fuck d'ya want?

IONA Holy SHIT is that one'a them Kylie Jenner / lip kits?

TOLLER DON'T TOUCH THAT

IONA I'd stab me own Ma ta get me hands on one'a these

TOLLER Wouldn't bother yourself Iona, most times I can't even tell if I'm lookin' at your arse or your face, seriously spit it out – why're ya here?

IONA *looks at* TOLLER, *then dives in for a bear hug.*

IONA Ah listen it's okay – I'm not goin' far

TOLLER AH JESUS

IONA I'll miss ya, ya know tha? Even though you've been a massive bitch these last few years – that stunt you pulled the last night was fuckin' low – but I forgive ya

TOLLER Miss me – tha fuck're ya talkin' about?

IONA I'm leavin' Toller – did ya not see me status and me snapchat and me insta story?

TOLLER No.

IONA Really?

TOLLER No cos I've no interest what you do with yourself.

TOLLER *notices the Crocs* **IONA**'s *wearing.*

What the fuck's that on your feet?

IONA Eh...fashion statement

TOLLER What's the statement? "I'm a total fuckin' wally?"
Why can't just ya just be normal for once?

IONA Yeh, me an' Pingu, movin' ta London, gonna be amazin'

TOLLER So...what – did ya think you were gonna come here,
we were gonna have a little cry together? Kiss an' make up?

IONA No I just want you ta know I'm gonna be a huge success
an' you're not.

TOLLER Where're you gonna live? I mean how're ya gonna pay
for all tha'? You're not even done with your Leavin' Cert,
what're ya gonna do for work? Have you actually thought
about anny of this?

IONA Eh YEH – Pingu's got ALL that taken care of.

TOLLER Righ' – cos my money's on you bein' homeless

IONA We're goin' ta stay with me Da alrigh'?

TOLLER You've not seen him since you were four Iona

IONA So? He's gonna be fuckin' thrilled ta see me. He's
fantastically wealthy.

TOLLER Where's he live?

Beat.

IONA We're gonna be social media influencers. We're gonna
have our own channel an' everythin'

TOLLER Jaysus

IONA Jaysus is righ' it's gonna be massive

TOLLER That place'll eat the pair'a ya alive

IONA Yeh well it's fuckin' better than here!

Beat, IONA *looks around* TOLLER*'s room and spots a pretty delectable pair of... Creepers.*

Nice runners

TOLLER Yeh pretty pleased with them I am.

IONA I want them back

TOLLER Touch them I'll burst you.

Beat.

IONA I feel sorry for ya ya know?

TOLLER Pfffff why?

IONA Bein' stuck here

Who from here has actually made it like?

TOLLER Eh, Conor McGregor

IONA Ah he barely lived here at all the fella's from Lucan.

Beat.

TOLLER Here Iona did you ever hear that expression – you can't polish a turd?

IONA Yeh

TOLLER Then what makes you think you're gonna be anny less of a huge fuckin' loser in London?

IONA What did I ever fuckin' do ta you, Toller? Really?

Beat. They stare each other down.

We used ta have *such* an amazin' time together

TOLLER ...You're righ'

IONA ...Hah?

TOLLER No, you're righ' ...

We did used ta...

I'm just remembering ehm

That time...

Oh my God, we must've been like...ten

That time...

TOLLER *cracks up.*

IONA *starts cracking up too.*

IONA Oh my God, what!?

TOLLER That time in primary you shat in a bin.

IONA THAT WASN'T ME I'VE TOLD YOU

TOLLER Definitely was

IONA Wasn't

TOLLER BIN... BIN... BIN...

IONA IT FUCKIN' WASN'T OKAY IT WASN'T EVERYONE'S
BEEN GIVIN' ME SHIT FOR YEARS ABOUT THAT AN'
IT WASN'T

IONA *has to take a moment.*

Well... Hah... This was a waste of fuckin' time –

Ya know Toller you've got me fuckin' wrong – really wrong

TOLLER Nope

IONA At least the lads've come to their fuckin' senses –

TOLLER Hah?

IONA At least your cousin's his head screwed on

TOLLER What, *Pockets*!?

IONA Sure Pockets AND Trix – they can't get enough of me

TOLLER Righ' an' I'm Kim Kardashian's left tit

IONA They're throwin' me a goin' away party an' all

TOLLER Iona, those lads barely know your name

IONA I mean if anythin' they're too keen like – fightin' them off I am – I think they want a slice of this cake, d'ya know what I'm sayin'?

TOLLER ...Trix?

IONA Yeh both'a them.

> **TOLLER** *is confounded by this news,* **IONA** *mistakes this for vulnerability.*

Yeh, that's righ'

I seen your little videos by the way.

You dance like a giraffe that's been shot in the kneecaps.

I'll be off will I? Have fun wit' your make-up, shame you've a face like a bag of mashed up shit an' all.

TOLLER What about your Mam?

IONA What do you care?

TOLLER ...She'll be heartbroken.

Scene Five
Quicker Than Shit From A Goose

PINGU*'s bedroom.* PINGU *is packing.*

IONA AHHHHHOWIYEEEE!!!

PINGU *jumps. How the hell did* IONA *get in?*

God this is excitin' isn't ih?

PINGU ...

IONA Here I'll give you a hand

IONA *folds some clothes up for* PINGU.

D'ya know what I can't wait ta raid? That ginormous Topshop – we'll get me Da ta take us on a shoppin' trip – Mam's always on about how much money he's sat on – we are gonna be decked OUT

OH – I was thinkin' we need ta get fake IDs so we can go clubbin' – I'm talkin' Ministry of Sound – I'm talkin' Wetherspoons – ntts-nttts-nttts-nttts-ntts-nttts

The pair of them pretend they're raving.

I cannot WAIT

They resume packing.

So eh... I did just want ta check –

Ya know that flight we were lookin' at for tomorrow evenin'?

PINGU ...

IONA You've not booked it yet have ya?

PINGU *pauses.*

I was just thinkin' like – so we're not rushin' – I mean it is a BIG move – just wondered if we wouldn't book the same one but like...a couple days later? Give us a bit of wiggle room ya know?

PINGU ...

IONA I just think it's more sensible. Don't wanna get there an' realise, ya know, we forgot our toothbrushes do we!?

PINGU ...

IONA Fine! You heard them they're gonna throw us a huge gaffer!!!

PINGU *dumps the items in their hands into their suitcase definitively.*

No need for a fuckin' tantrum! It's two days it's not a big deal!!!!

Ah come on we've wanted this for fuckin' years!

PINGU ...

IONA Ah they weren't ignorin' ya!

PINGU *makes it clear they are done with that lot. They resume packing.*

Please!!!! I just want a taste of it before we go! I just want ta fuckin' show them they were fuckin' wrong about us this whole fuckin' time – that we are the life an' fuckin' soul! Don't you want that? Ta fuckin' show them who we are??

PINGU *stops packing and looks at* **IONA**.

I'd do anythin' for ya – I'm just askin' this one thing

Two days.

Two little days!!!

An' then we are gonna be outta here quicker than shit from a goose alrigh'? Promise.

Eventually, **PINGU** *resumes packing. It's a no.*

A while. Re-strategising. Then:

Give us time ta leave Toller a fuckin' sick leavin' gift, wa?

PINGU *pauses.*

Somethin' real grim, give her nightmares the rest of her life?

PINGU *looks at* **IONA.**

Go-wan ya good thing

Scene Six
A Hamster Utopia

POCKETS' *house.* POCKETS *and* IONA *enter the bedroom.*

POCKETS *(to offstage)* YOU'RE A PRICK, YA KNOW THA'?
Thick fuckin' cunt – sorry – he's a fuckin' –

IONA I wish I'd a brother

POCKETS Honestly ya don't

IONA Ya look a lot alike

Well – he looks like he'd crush a car between his teeth but
similar enough yeah

Beat. It dawns on them that they barely know each other.

POCKETS I was kinda countin' on showin' ya the telly so eh

Bit messy in here sorry

IONA *spots a laptop and rushes over to it.*

IONA Oh my God is this a MacBook Pro? Does it have the
touchpad an' everythin'!?

POCKETS MIND –

POCKETS *hurries over and snatches it from her.*

Sorry – me Da'd murder me if I broke it

IONA That's a fair aul pair of tits isn't it?
What. Is. THAT?

She is pointing to a hamster cage.

POCKETS Oh *fuck* eh –

He tries to throw a blanket over the cage but it's too late.

IONA Is that a hamster!!??

POCKETS Eh yeh look ignore tha' – here grab the MacBook there –

IONA *has already reached inside and is pulling Benny out.*

CAREFUL – eh – just be careful with him.

IONA WHAT IS ITS NAME?

POCKETS eh...that's Benny.

IONA BENNY!

POCKETS Hah...yeah

Silence a while as **IONA** *strokes and lets Benny run over her hands as* **POCKETS** *watches.*

Right will we eh

Will we put him away now?

IONA Eh NO – can we build him a run?

POCKETS Eh

IONA Ah g'wan g'wan g'wan g'wan g'wan g'wan

POCKETS Eh yeh alrigh'

You're gas ya know that?

IONA Sorry what dya mean by 'gas'?

POCKETS Eh

IONA Like good or bad?

POCKETS Eh good – yeh, good good

IONA Oh...okay

Great

POCKETS Righ' eh...

POCKETS *goes round the room gathering bits and bobs, some more cardboard loo roll and kitchen roll centres, whatever.*

IONA Jesus it's like Christmas

POCKETS *grabs Benny's hamster ball and they pop him in and get to work as Benny rolls around having the time of his life.*

Dunno *where* Pingu got ta – they'd *love* this

POCKETS Pingu's comin'?

IONA Well yeah! Pingu loves a big telly!

POCKETS Here ya must be dead excited are ya?

IONA I'm not just excited I am overwhelmed to have met Benny

POCKETS No – about goin'

IONA Oh eh

Yeh – Yeh I mean course I am it's a whole new start like yeh

Beat.

Here where'd ya get Benny?

POCKETS Ahhh... I'm just mindin' him for someone.

Beat.

Thanks for comin' over like – great ta have ya

IONA Thanks for havin' me! I was fuckin' thrilled when ya text me!

...I mean if I'm bein' honest I'm proper shittin' it about goin'

POCKETS Ah they'll be lucky ta have ya Iona

IONA *beams. It's almost become too genuine, neither of them know where to look.*

Yeh I went out with an English girl once. Yeh she was mad uptight. They can be a bit like that ya know.

IONA Right...yeh

They work in silence.

Your Da away is he?

POCKETS Yeh

IONA Is it true he works for the Monk?

POCKETS ...We don't really talk about ih

IONA But...you've got a MacBook Pro, a huge telly, a PS4 an' a cabinet full of waterford crystal –

POCKETS Have we?

IONA Yeh

My gaff's a fuckin' wreck

I've wanted a hamster since God was a boy, desperate for one

Me Ma won't let me

She's a bit of a Debbie Downer ta be honest

She's a nurse but I can't say much for her bedside manner now

ANYWAY point is I'd probably trade me own Ma ta get a hamster like Benny, he's class

POCKETS Gas – good gas

Where've ya been hiding Iona?

They work in silence.

I got Benny when me cousin died.

It was his, like – Benny.

IONA How'd he die?

POCKETS *doesn't respond.*

They work in silence.

Sorry

...

Pockets, I'm really sorry

Don't be annoyed wit' me

...

I didn't mean ta –

There's a knock on the door.

POCKETS I TOLD YA YOU CAN HAVE THE MAIN ROOM –
'sake –

POCKETS *yanks open the door. It's* **PINGU**.

IONA Pingu!!!

POCKETS Oh

IONA LOOK what we're doin' Pockets has a HAMSTER called
BENNY
Come in! Why're ya standin' there like a fuckin' lemon?

POCKETS Here why don't we all go down the park get a few
cans in or somethin'?

PINGU *indicates it's time to go.*

IONA Ah we've only barely started! Get stuck in pal!

Both have to concede to **IONA**'s *wide-eyed joy.* **PINGU**
steps uneasily into the room. **POCKETS** *eyes* **PINGU** *up.*

So this is Benny. He's...how old?

POCKETS I dunno as I said – not mine

IONA Let's just say a year old. He's a Capricorn. And he's
desperately going ta miss me when I go, aren't ya?

POCKETS Course he will – sure we all will – there'll be an Iona
shaped hole in Crumlin when you've gone.

IONA Ah shtop

POCKETS Jaysis if you were stayin' ...
I'd buy ya a whole fuckin' zoo so I would.

IONA Wouldja?

POCKETS Jesus yeh, you'd have a fleet of Bennys, a whole fuckin'
crew

IONA Fuck that's the dream

POCKETS Sure you deserve it babes

POCKETS *puts his arm around* IONA, *maybe chances a kiss.*

PINGU *knocks something or drops something, pulling focus. The moment's gone.*

POCKETS *shoots* PINGU *a look.*

IONA Would ya buy Pingu a hamster too?

POCKETS Ehhh...

IONA Like if Pingu was stayin' as well?

POCKETS Eh yeh, sure

IONA An' what would you call him Pingu?

PINGU *indicates it would be Benny to* IONA.

Benny

POCKETS Ya can't call him Benny, Benny's called Benny

PINGU's *poker face is impervious.*

I'm serious Benny is Benny

You not got packin' ta do or somethin'?

PINGU *shrugs.*

(to IONA*)* You know...if you were stayin' we could do allsorts together –

IONA Yeh?

POCKETS – Parties – serious craic – ah man we'd seriously make up for lost time, wha?

IONA Ah, now – are ya hearin' this!? Snake charmer here, Jesus!

POCKETS I mean ih. I think you're beautiful, Iona.

IONA *melts.*

The moment is highly charged.

PINGU *knocks a lamp over making a huge fuss.*

POCKETS *is raging.*

The moment's gone.

Fuck it – POCKETS *goes to kiss* IONA *again but –.*

IONA Ah I think you gave Benny a fright he's just shat on my hand

POCKETS Ach Iona – I hate ta see ya leave but I love ta watch ya go

IONA Ah shtop

IONA *hurries out.* PINGU *goes to follow* IONA.

POCKETS Eh...pretty sure she can wipe her own arse pal

PINGU *halts. Puts their poker face on ready to stay.*

Long beat between POCKETS *and* PINGU.

(re. Benny) Not a fuckin' word.

Pause. POCKETS *crosses his arms so it just so happens to push his biceps out impressively.*

Here PINGU's *responses – except when they laugh at* POCKETS *– are near impossible to read.*

Great girl isn't she?

Yeh great girl.

We could be mates, Pingu

This gives something PINGU *to laugh about.*

Think you're better than us here do ya?

You know, I was born in this house.

I've lived my whole life in the Old County Glen estate an' I don't plan on leavin' til they carry me out.

Everyone within' in a twenty mile radius knows my family name – they know ta give it the respect it deserves.

I'm proud of bein' from this place and what I don't like is you givin' it the finger.

PINGU *just stares at* POCKETS.

What is goin' on in that head of yours hah?

Be easier just ta say somethin', no? Cos this whole...thing... it's not cool, or interesting by the way. It's fuckin' weird is what it is.

Benny saunters by in his ball.

Friends tell each other things, don't they?

Yeh. Things like.

How I've slept with at least thirty motts.

Yeh I'd say about thirty, maybe forty.

What about yourself?

PINGU *just stares.*

Give me a clue here Pingu...

What's your fuckin' deal? Hah?

Cos you're cockblockin' me bigtime here an' it is seriously startin' ta get on my wick

Benny rolls by in his ball. PINGU *stops the ball with their foot.*

Can ya take yer foot off Benny's ball please?

PINGU *doesn't move.*

See, Benny's a good mate. Cos he's helpin' like.

But if Benny fucked with me

PINGU *raises a foot as if to stamp on Benny – a test.*

POCKETS *dives for Benny.*

Here stop tha'! Jesus

POCKETS *clutches Benny in his little ball to his chest.*

Fuckin' nut job

Well that was illuminating.

Doesn't seem that mad about your trip. Iona.

PINGU's *poker face drops, just for a second.*

Yeh made it clear enough you're basically draggin' her ta London

IONA *re-enters.*

IONA I wonder how Benny'd feel if I took a shit on him, wa'?

What's wrong?

I'm not actually gonna do ih!

Scene Seven
This Is My Turf

The toilet in Matt the Rashers.

PINGU has just entered. They go to shut the door but just as they do– a foot appears, jamming it.

Soon a whole body is trying to squeeze in as PINGU wrestles with the door– it is TOLLER. They struggle. TOLLER wins and slips in, locking the door behind her.

TOLLER What? You came in here ta piss didntcha?

PINGU doesn't move.

Gwan sit or stand, we're all dyin' ta know what y'are

PINGU grabs the emergency cable.

You pull that emergency cable I'll give you a real fuckin' emergency, I'm serious

PINGU doesn't move.

You get me banned from Matt the Rashers I'll end you.

PINGU doesn't move.

HELLO? You really know how ta fuck me off don'tcha? Matt the Rashers is *my* haunt. I just asked Cathy out there if she'd any rashers and sausages left and what'd she do? Points over at you. Tells me you got the last of ih. I don't care if this is some kind of last supper or what but you need ta stop wit' your shit *now*.

PINGU puts their hand on their tummy as to indicate – yes omg that meal was delicious.

Who do you think you are?

You know I could get Pockets an' Trix down here ta batter you right now if I wanted?

PINGU *is the epitome of outward calm.*

Are you hearin' what I'm sayin'!?

PINGU *is so impervious it rattles* TOLLER.

I'm gonna say this once: you tell Iona to stop whatever shit she's tryin' ta pull and the both of ya fuck off ta London NOW alrigh'?

No hangin' around wit' MY mates, no party – NOW

Clear?

Suddenly PINGU *looks like they're going to be sick. They kind of cough. Hunch over a bit. Put their hands to their mouth.*

What the... What's wrong wit' you?

It's like PINGU*'s coughing and puking up an alien.*

...Shit

Are ya okay?

Just as TOLLER*'s got a bit worried,* PINGU *finally proverbially spits it out...it's the finger!!! Fuck you.*

Seriously? You gonna talk ta ME like tha'? You'd wanna remember your place

PINGU *takes out their phone and plays* TOLLER *a video of* IONA *and* POCKETS *from yesterday (the Benny scene). It's* POCKETS *saying goodbye to* IONA *and giving her a huge hug, "See ya tomorrow gorgeous"// "Can't wait!".*

There's no way that can be real

PINGU *plays another clip.*

That's not real

PINGU *shrugs – nope!*

It's not – it's not real – Pocket's never let her in the door

PINGU *shrugs. A moment where* TOLLER, *shook, reformulates, puts on her most terrifying mask.*

You carry on, I'll make you fuckin' WISH you'd gone ta London yesterday.

PINGU *is impervious.*

TOLLER *makes to go.*

Safe trip bitch.

PINGU *waves...buh bye.*

TOLLER *goes.*

Exhausted from holding their head so high, PINGU *tries to breathe, tries to stop their hands shaking. We spend a moment with them.*

Scene Eight
A Warning

IONA*'s house – hall-cum-living room.*

TOLLER*'s tried to plaster her face in makeup but a bruise is becoming visible despite that.*

TOLLER God this place looks exactly the same

IONA You an interior designer now?

TOLLER No just...like goin' back in time is all.

IONA Yeh well we're not made a money so

TOLLER Nor are we

IONA Yeh but your uncle is so no point pretendin'

Beat.

Well what d'ya want?

TOLLER You an' –

IONA Ya fancy me dontcha, that's why ya couldn't be around me – everyone fuckin' fancies me these days

TOLLER Fuck no

IONA I wouldn't judge ya if ya did, I'm a ride

TOLLER I strongly do not fancy you

IONA You're repressin' somethin' I can tell

TOLLER I'll be repressin' you in a minute!

I came ta say: I can't wait for you ta fuck off ta London –

IONA That's exactly what we're doin' – serious thick head on ya, ya know tha'?

TOLLER Ah why dontcha fuck off like your Dad?

IONA HOW did you become such a rotten bitch?

Cos I swear you were actually good craic when we were kids

We created a SHRINE ta the Jonas Brothers together – it's on my bedroom wall upstairs –

I've still fuckin' got it!

An' ever since we hit secondary...you been walkin' round like your shit didn't stink

You broke my fuckin' heart.

And I want ta know why. WHY.

TOLLER Iona get over it alright! Ya need ta move on! Everyone else has! It's called growing up!

Things fuckin' change!

Silence.

IONA I used ta wake up every day so fuckin' scared about comin' inta school I'd be sick in me bag on the bus. Because a you.

I used ta picture meself stamping on your stupid little face every time you pretended you didn't hear me tryin' ta talk ta ya in class

TOLLER Does this not give you an idea / why I –

IONA I used ta fantasise about pullin' your stupid ponytail out from the roots... Peelin' your scalp right back from your skull

Banging on the door.

TRIX IONA!

POCKETS IONA PET LET US IN IT'S AN EMERGENCY

IONA *opens the door and the lads rush in, out of breath.*

TRIX What're you doin' here?

TOLLER What're *you* doin' here!?

TRIX This is a fuckin' emergency lads

POCKETS We need ta motor, Pingu's fuckin' followin' us

IONA Followin'?

POCKETS Nothin's happened ya has ih?

TRIX Nutball, fuckin' nutball

IONA What are ya talkin' abou'?

POCKETS Pingu

TRIX Ah Pingu man

IONA WHAT ABOUT PINGU?

POCKETS JUST STANDIN' THERE

TRIX Terrifyin'

POCKETS Righ' outside me window

TOLLER What?

TRIX Right outside

POCKETS Starin' in at me

TRIX We're there playin' PS4 – outside the window – starin'

POCKETS Proper psycho eyes

TRIX Killer eyes that's righ' – proper starin'

POCKETS Out for blood

TRIX So we leg it righ'

POCKETS Didn't feel safe

TRIX Felt watched

POCKETS Head up ta Texas Fried Chicken see if we can find you

TRIX We're worried like, Pingu's obviously snapped or somethin'

POCKETS Definitely snapped – kinda crazed look about them ya know?

TRIX An' Pingu starts followin' us

POCKETS Yeh so like we start runnin'

TRIX An' Pingu starts runnin'

POCKETS Minute later, I spot Doyler drivin' past in his Honda flag him down

TRIX Yeh we hop in righ' – Pingu starts runnin' after the car

POCKETS Tries ta jump on the back

TRIX Honestly like the fuckin' Terminator

POCKETS Misses, obviously, so we got away like but...

TRIX Those eyes – man – gives me the shivers so it does

POCKETS Proper heebie jeebies

IONA I only saw Pingu this mornin'

TRIX Obviously snapped since then

POCKETS Snapped.

TOLLER Wait a second, so Pingu turns up at yours, gives you a funny look an' now yiz are shittin' yourselves?

TRIX D'ya not hear that Terminator bit?

POCKETS I'm serious – it takes a lot ta scare me an' I was rattled

TOLLER Why?

POCKETS Hah?

TOLLER Why Pingu do tha'?

POCKETS Doesn't want us hangin' out wit' Iona shur

TRIX Tryin' ta sabotage our friendship

IONA No – no Pingu wouldn't do tha'

TOLLER Fuck sake, no *way*

POCKETS Here what's with the mouth on you today? D'ya wanna shut up or wha'?

IONA I might just go and find –

IONA *makes to head out.*

POCKETS Honestly wouldn't go out there

TRIX At least let Pingu cool down a bit first

POCKETS Ya know what I *always* knew there was somethin' *really* fucked up about Pingu

TOLLER *(to* **IONA***)* You're not buyin' all this are ya?

TRIX We're tellin' the fuckin' truth!

POCKETS Toller I'm really about ta lose me rag wit' you.

> **TRIX** *engulfs* **IONA** *in a hug.*

TRIX Ah you're alrigh', we'll look after ya pet

POCKETS C'mere ta me pet – he's not showered today

TRIX Yer okay, we won't let anything happen to ya

IONA You sure bout all this?

> **POCKETS** *takes* **IONA** *square by the shoulders and looks into her eyes.*

POCKETS Would I ever lie to you?

> *Beat.*

TOLLER Fuck sake

POCKETS Okay – time ta go –

TOLLER They're movin' together!

TRIX Sorry since when did you give a shit?

TOLLER I *don't* give a / shit but –

TRIX The *neck* of you then –

TOLLER Fuck you Trix!

TRIX An' I will never fuck you Toller.
That's the point.

> *Deeply stung,* **TOLLER** *sees no choice but to go.*

Here look, we weren't gonna say this before cos I knew ye were good mates but like, honestly we always liked ya

POCKETS Oh yeh always did

TRIX It was only Pingu we'd a problem with

POCKETS Always in the way

TRIX You woulda been at ALL the gaffers an' all

POCKETS Just didn't want Pingu there

TRIX *Always* thought you were class though didn't we?

IONA ...really?

POCKETS Oh yeh, from day one

TRIX Kills me to think – how different it all coulda been

POCKETS What – if Pingu hadn't been in the equation?

TRIX Well yeh

That not kill you a bit?

IONA *puts her head in her hands.*

POCKETS So look – we thought you might be a bit upset so we've got somethin' ta cheer you up –

TRIX That gaff party we promised ya?

POCKETS Well get ready cos it's goin' down – TONIGH'

IONA ...Yeah, it's just

...I'm sorry lads I just

POCKETS Ah get a few tins in ya you'll be righ' as rain!

TRIX Few tunes!

POCKETS *takes* **IONA**'s *hand and pulls her up.*

POCKETS Iona – this is the party you deserve – for all them parties you missed – cos' a Pingu – for all them times yokes like Toller wouldn't let ya in – for all those times all of us were too stupid ta see how great you really are

And you are *great*

Tonight is gonna be the gaffer to end all gaffers, an' it is gonna be all about YOU.

Every minute of it.

You ready babes?

Coda:

PINGU's *house:*

PINGU *is under the covers watching* **PINGU** *cartoons.*

They stare at their suitcase. Fuck it.

They book the flight.

At the same time...

POCKETS' *back garden,* **TRIX**, **POCKETS**, *and* **IONA**.

TRIX *throws* **IONA** *and* **POCKETS** *a can each. They each pierce a hole in the side of their can.*

TRIX   Get that inta ya!

ALL   YA SLUT YA!

They put their mouths to the cans and glug.

Scene Nine
She's A Gas Bitch

The party.

TRIX No listen! – CREXIT: The Campaign for an Independent Self-Governing State of Crumlin, independent of mainland Ireland and most definitely nothing ta do with the English –

IONA Sign me up!

POCKETS Stupid

IONA Is this specifically about trade agreements or more generally ta do with our national sense of self?

TRIX I'm glad you asked – let me tell you what life would be like under an Independent, Sovereign State of Crumlin –

POCKETS Iona don't mind him –

TRIX Crumlin post-Crexit: It is a *paradise* – imagine Crumlin now – already the best four square miles in Ireland hands down – but about eighty million times BETTER than THAT –

POCKETS Not even possible

TRIX Crumlin post-Crexit is a Utopia saved only for Ireland's good and great, its best and brightest –

IONA So Twink is there!

TRIX Twink is definitely there – Bono

TOLLER *enters, surprised to see them all hammering the cans.*

TOLLER What's this?

TRIX What're you doin' here?

IONA There she is! Welcome! We are prelashin' for my HUGE PARTY. You might wanna get yourself cleaned up for it babes you're lookin' a bit crusty.

TOLLER *(to the lads)* Seriously?

IONA Oh wait – YOU'RE NOT INVITED

TOLLER YOU texted me ta come here!

(to **POCKETS***)* Your Da'll have your scalp

TRIX Did we ask your permission granny?

TOLLER I'll tell him!

POCKETS Don't forget what we done for you in this family –

TRIX EH! I'M IN THE MIDDLE OF SOMETHIN' HERE!

IONA YEAH TOLLER SHUT THE FUCK UP

TOLLER Are you drunk!?

IONA Eh... YES!

TRIX A MANIFESTO FOR AN INDEPENDENT SOVEREIGN STATE OF CRUMLIN – the laws are strict but fair: no fat motts in leggings. Toller – no more drawin' your eyebrows on with a Sharpie –

TOLLER Ah fuck off!

TRIX State subsidised chicken fillet rolls –

IONA YES

TOLLER ...not drawn on with fucking Sharpie...

TRIX Free iPhones – no more school – twenty four hour parties with enough Mandy to put a smile on the face of every man woman and child in Crumlin – everyone gets a swish car – green lambos to be precise – anyone who passes in or out of the area must pay a toll, with all the money goin' towards a monument to McGregor, a statue twelve feet tall and so lifelike motts will be caught at all hours tryin ta score the face off it –

IONA SAVAGE!

TOLLER This is the stupidest thing I ever fuckin' heard

TRIX You're not welcome in the Independent Sovereign State of Crumlin then so

IONA HA!!

TOLLER Ah go choke on a biscuit ya scaldy bitch

TRIX Now: I'm your benevolent leader – a bit like the Monk –

POCKETS What d'*you* know about the bleedin' Monk, jaysus –

TRIX – Kind and reasonable at the best of times, but if you cross me I'll slaughter your whole family without hesitation, but also a deft hand at negotiating favourable trade agreements with mainland Ireland –

POCKETS *(to IONA)* – we all know I'd be runnin' the show – wouldn't I?

TRIX Iona– if you'll join me

> IONA *leaps up with a pointed look at* TOLLER.

Now, this here is the governess of the Independent Sovereign State of Crumlin, Iona Hanratty, style icon, walking dictionary and absolute ride –

IONA *(to TOLLER:)* Hear that!?

TOLLER Christ

IONA Lads I am havin' the BEST time – okay I'm serious lads, how can we make Crexit happen, who do I need to write ta?

> PINGU *enters.*

There you fuckin' are!

POCKETS What're you doing here?

TRIX Did you invite Pingu?

TOLLER No

IONA I did! We've a full house now!

You're gonna bring the fun, aren'tcha pal? Cos THIS IS FUCKIN' IT!

Coda:

The party ramps up eight gears or so. **IONA** *is on cloud nine, the centre of attention.*

Bass – Drinking – Dancing – The Craic.

TOLLER *sits moodily sipping a can.*

PINGU *awkwardly tries to look like they're having fun.*

TRIX *hands out naggins "Nagginnnnsssrs". They swig.*

IONA *gets her phone out.*

IONA ARE YOU LISTENIN' CRUMLIN!? YOU'D BETTER GET YOUR BUTTS DOWN HERE FOR A GOOD TIME WHA'?

They all cluster in, passing the camera around.

TRIX HOWIYEEEEE! WE ARE GONNA GET POLLUTED TONIGHT!

IONA – it tastes like paint stripper –

POCKETS YEOOOOWWW!!!!!!

IONA PINGU LOVES A PARTY WA!?

Ah wouldya crack a fuckin' smile!? This is it Pingu! We're here!!!

...Could ya not even just fuckin' try?

TRIX Here let's see ya neck tha'!

IONA No way!

TRIX Yes way! Do ih!

A pause in time as they all neck their vodka.

IONA Here have a sip of this – if you can get past the horrendous taste it's unreal I'm tellin' ya –

PINGU *is really not keen.*

Ah come ON!!!

TRIX Gwan just a little taste!

IONA Why'd ya come if you were only gonna piss on me fire?

TRIX It's like we told ya –

But **PINGU** *takes* **IONA** *by the wrist and pulls her aside.*

POCKETS Iona –

PINGU *gets their phone out to show* **IONA** *the tickets but before they can –.*

IONA Why're ya doin' this?

PINGU ...

IONA Why d'ya have ta begrudge me this one bit of happiness!?

PINGU ...

IONA Chasin' the lads, makin' them think I can't be friends with them – an' now this!

PINGU ...

IONA Stop actin' like ya don't know, ya do know!

PINGU *manages to get* **IONA** *to look at the screen.*

What's this?

YA BOOKED IH?

PINGU ...

IONA Tomorrow night?

PINGU *nods excitedly. They do not get the reaction they expect.*

TOLLER What's goin' on?

IONA None of your fuckin' business.

IONA *peels away from* **PINGU** *in search of another can.* **PINGU** *stares after* **IONA,** *confused, worried.*

TRIX Here Iona – you've eh – you've somethin' on your face

IONA Do I?

TRIX Here I'll get ih

> TRIX *rubs an imaginary smudge from* IONA*'s cheek.*
> *His hand lingers as he checks her out. This is it. This*
> *is him trying to go in for the kill.*

POCKETS A toast! IONA! She's leaving us for a shithole where
they don't even have chicken fillet rolls –

IONA WHAT!?

POCKETS Or a clear plan for Brexit!

IONA No seriously do they not have chicken fillet rolls?

TRIX Ah she's a gas bitch!

POCKETS You're a gem Iona: I'm not even jus' sayin' tha', you're
bleedin' brilliant

TRIX Here here! You're a class act Iona!

POCKETS We wish you were stayin' don't we!

TRIX STAY! STAY! STAY! STAY!

POCKETS STAY! STAY! STAY! / STAY! STAY!

IONA God I wish I was staying

> I WISH I WAS STAYING AN' WE COULD DO THIS EVERY
> FUCKIN DAY!!!!

POCKETS WEEEEYYYY!!!!!!

> *The lads rush* IONA *and hug her, maybe someone puts her*
> *on their shoulders, the music turns up, they're passing*
> *round cans.*

> PINGU *goes into the house.*

IONA HERE LET ME PUT THIS ON ME STORIES! WHERE
IS EVERYONE, THE PARTY'S OVER HERE WA!

PINGU *returns with a glass of water. They push through the lads, hold* IONA *steady and try to hand her the glass.*

What's tha'?

Water? What do I want tha' for?

POCKETS You're bein' a real buzzkill ya know tha'?

PINGU *is nonplussed, they offer* IONA *the glass again.*

IONA You're alrigh'

TOLLER Drink it Iona you're locked

IONA Okay lads are we not sick of her comin' in here tellin' us what ta do?

TOLLER Excuse me!? The fuckin' cheek!!!!

IONA I'll tell you what's fuckin' cheek – you paradin' around in them Creepers. They're mine.

POCKETS Are they?

IONA They sure as fuck are

POCKETS Toller – hand them over

TOLLER I will in my hole

IONA He said HAND THEM OVER.

TOLLER Make me.

IONA *looks at the two lads. She clicks her fingers.*

The boys take TOLLER *by each arm and lift her off the floor.*

GET THE FUCK OFF ME!

IONA *swans over and pulls the runners off* TOLLER'*s feet.*

IONA Tanks very much

TOLLER ARSEHOLES!

The lads put **TOLLER** *down. She goes to rush* **IONA** *but the lads block her path.*

With a look **POCKETS** *makes it clear to her she'd better leave.*

IONA HOW DO *YOU* LIKE IT YA MANKY BITCH! THIS IS MY TURF NOW WA'?

PINGU *is back again with the water.*

I *told* ya –

PINGU ...

IONA I SAID YOU'RE ALRIGH' FUCK'S SAKE

A stand off. **IONA** *looks* **PINGU** *dead in the eye and skulls the can.* **PINGU** *tries to pull it off her.*

Get off!

IONA *pulls the can away and bats the glass of water all over* **PINGU**. **PINGU** *stands, dripping, as* **TRIX** *and* **POCKETS** *break into laughter.*

POCKETS Oh shit!!!

TRIX Fuck! Brutal!

TRIX *gets his phone out to capture the moment. Suddenly, in the moment, buoyed by the laughter,* **IONA** *pours her can of beer all down* **PINGU**. *The boys can't believe it – they explode into laughter.*

PINGU, *once what has happened has truly sunk in, goes to retaliate, incensed.*

But the boys are too quick and block **PINGU** *from reaching* **IONA**. **IONA** *is literally protected by the human barrier they create.*

IONA This was the ONE THING – the *one* thing I asked for and ya had ta ruin it

You know they woulda been my friend? If it hadn't been for you

POCKETS She's right ya know.

TRIX You've really held her back

IONA Cos you're weird

TRIX You are weird, I can confirm that.

IONA Go home Pingu

POCKETS You heard her

They're not leaving, their quiet resolution is unsettling.

IONA Don't you *dare* look at me like tha' – I'm allowed enjoy meself!

TRIX *(to* **IONA***)* It's them psycho eyes we were tellin' you about

POCKETS What is wrong wit' you?

PINGU *doesn't move.*

IONA HOW can I go ta London wit' ya when I can't even trust ya?

POCKETS Seriously now – what's your deal?

TRIX Can I ask – why're you called Pingu?

POCKETS No – I want ta know – what's your real name?

IONA GO HOME

POCKETS What *are* you?

TRIX Yeh pick a side, ya know?

Long beat, **IONA** *and* **PINGU** *stare each other down.*

IONA *hardens.*

IONA *(to the boys)* You wanna know do ya? What they are? *(to* **PINGU***)* I fuckin' will

PINGU *begs* **IONA.**

Here lads

D'ya wanna hear somethin' funny?

*IONA stares at PINGU. PINGU shakes their head. This
only makes IONA more resolute.*

C'mere

She pulls POCKETS to her and whispers in his ear.

POCKETS ...Really?

IONA Yeh.

*PINGU still stays resolute. They can withstand it. They
can. They can.*

TRIX Here Iona –

*But IONA is focused on PINGU, whose heart is breaking
in slow motion.*

IONA You look at *me* like tha'?

You don't *know* me.

*IONA shoots PINGU a look but just as quickly she's turned
away and cracks another can.*

TRIX Iona – what'd she –

IONA There. Done.

Let's get back to the fuckin' party.

*Their heart breaking in slow motion, PINGU finally
leaves.*

TRIX is still filming.

TRIX Well that was some craic wasn't ih? Didn't see that comin' –
not complainin' – jus' didn't see it comin'. Here what did
ya say ta Pockets there? For the camera

IONA walks over and slams a jamming track on.

IONA LADS – FELLAS – LET'S NOT FORGET WHOSE PARTY IT IS!

POCKETS COURSE NOT!

TRIX YEOOOWW!!!!

IONA gets her phone out and does a live story.

IONA NO ONE FUCKS WITH IONA HANRATTY – YA HEAR? NO ONE

POCKETS Iona you fuckin' *legend*

TRIX Yeah *total* legend –

POCKETS That was amazin' –

IONA You're amazin' Pockets

You're a fuckin' *ride* ya know tha'?

Beat. Then **IONA** *positively lobs the gob at* **POCKETS**.

TRIX *slowly lowers his phone.*

Then he crushes the can in his hand and dumps it on the floor.

His expression hardens.

ACT TWO

Coda:

Night.

We join **PINGU**, *raw, still shaking, in pain.*

They wipe beer off themselves.

They do their utmost to calm themselves, clenching and unclenching their fists.

Counting their breaths.

Finally they come to total, complete stillness.

A smallness.

Scene Ten
Ya Flaccid Fuck Ya

That night, after the party. 5am, both frazzled.

POCKET's *bedroom.* **POCKETS** *is on the bed.*

POCKETS Told ya my parties were legendary wa?

IONA It was UNRALE!

POCKETS That's a send off ya won't quick forget?

IONA ...Yeah...

POCKETS What? What's wrong?

IONA I mean

Can't exactly go London now can I? Not exactly in Pingu's good books

Not that I even want ta go wit' Pingu sure you saw yourself they're no craic!

POCKETS Sure fuck Pingu – you don't need them – it's *your* Da your stayin' wit'

IONA Yeah...

POCKETS Isn't ih?

IONA Oh yeah

POCKETS Here – what *is* Pingu's deal? Why were ya mates so long?

IONA Deal?

POCKETS All the gear an' the hair an' all?

Why say nothin'? Even when, ya know, just fuckin' sayin' something'd solve all your fuckin' problems?

IONA ...Pingu got sick of havin' ta always...

Ta always defend themself

Like defend...not bein' a girl or a boy

POCKETS Eh yeh but Pingu *is* a –

IONA No. Pingu is Pingu.

POCKETS You said yourself –

IONA ...

POCKETS Then why were they hiding being –

IONA Pingu wasn't hiding anything.

POCKETS Look either way, why be lettin' people talk shit about ya an' not snap back ya know?

IONA Pingu didn't want ta always be...like explainin' themselves ta people

You know, Pingu'd say... "I'm this" an' people'd just be like "Eh no you're not" an' it's tirin'

So when they moved here for secondary they just stopped talkin' –

POCKETS I mean would ya not toughen up like?

IONA Well look sure I'm best shot of Pingu they were holdin' me back

Awkward beat.

POCKETS C'mere

...Not *that* scary am I?

POCKETS *envelops her in a hug...*

IONA You're actually a fuckin kitten arentcha?

POCKETS*'first instinct is to get defensive, but he quickly softens realising it's a joke.*

POCKETS Yeh big fluffy fuckin' marshmallow me

IONA If only people knew it, heart a' gold under all that muscle hah?

POCKETS You're right about the muscle wha?

IONA What's it feel like ta batter someone?

POCKETS Jesus ya don't hold back do ya?

IONA Why's everyone always sayin' it like it's a bad fuckin' thing!

POCKETS ...sorry

I dunno eh

I mean I've helped me big brother train since I could walk so it just comes natural like

IONA I'm only askin' cos I'm thinkin' a takin' up bare knuckle fightin'. You could train me up.

POCKETS Yeh?

IONA Yeh so everyone knows and fears my name – and my fists

POCKETS You're an eejit ya know tha'?

...

Blitzin' anyone in London who looks at ya funny eh?

IONA ...Ach

Would *you* come?

POCKETS Ta London? Me?

IONA Yeh

Maybe **POCKETS** *seriously considers it for a moment.*

Beat.

POCKETS Ah no

IONA Why not?

POCKETS ...

IONA What's here for ya?

Beat.

POCKETS Everythin'.

They sit a minute.

I'll miss ya ya know tha'?

IONA Will ya!?

POCKETS Course

Course I will.

He kisses her.

She kisses back.

Things get hot and heavy pretty quick.

IONA *halts proceedings.*

IONA Sorry eh

Nothin' sorry

They continue.

IONA *pushes* POCKETS *off.*

Here listen I know I probably seem like I really know what I'm doin' and I've had loads of cock an' tha' but I've actually no fuckin' clue what I'm doin'

POCKETS *has to laugh.*

I'm just sayin' ya know I don't want ta be accused of false advertisin' or anything – like I'm pretty sure I'll be amazin' at sex but there's no guarantees like that's all I'm sayin' so keep your expectations low and let yourself be pleasantly surprised okay?

POCKETS Oh my god you are fuckin' gas

IONA Gas in a good way?

POCKETS Gas in a good way.

You're grand. Relax.

IONA Okay totally relaxed now.

Thank you.

As you were.

Things once again get hot and heavy.

After a short while... IONA looks down.

Is it?

POCKETS Yeh, hold on, hold on

Just

Can ya –

IONA Oh...yeh

She reaches down to give him a hand.

POCKETS It's never hap –

Ya know

Never usually eh –

IONA Oh, yeh, no, yeh course, God, don't worry

POCKETS Yeah, it's just—so upset you're goin' like

IONA Yeh yeh course – yeh

They fumble, both concentrating hard.

Is it...?

POCKETS I don't I don't it's usually

I dunno it

Like cos I know I'm losin' ya

It just won't –

IONA Ah no you're fine / that's sweet I –

POCKETS No, should be / any second –

IONA Do you have a problem?

POCKETS No, course I fuckin' don't I'm just fuckin' me heart
is broken over everythin' ya know it's

IONA It's ok, we don't / have to

POCKETS NO IT'S FINE IT'LL / BE FINE

IONA Okay, okay –

POCKETS Just, just put your hand –

IONA Okay –

...Are ya sure ya don't want to / try this another –

POCKETS Just – OH COME ON

IONA Calm down, it's –

POCKETS STOP SAYIN' IT'S OK IT'S NOT OK

IONA Yer upset, it's –

POCKETS WHY WON'T IT FUCKIN' – JESUS CHRIST – HOLD
ON – HOLD ON

POCKETS *pulls his phone out and brings up some porn
and plays it, focusing on the screen as he tries to sort
himself out.* IONA *just lies there.*

It doesn't work.

JESUS FUCK

IONA We can – it's okay we can do it another time –

POCKETS WHEN? WHEN OTHER TIME, IONA? / YOU'RE
FUCKIN' LEAVIN' –

POCKETS *starts thumping the pillow by* IONA*'s head.*

JESUS FUCK JESUS FUCKING CHRIST AFTER / ALL
THIS

IONA Look we don't have ta do it now –

POCKETS GOD I'm – can you – can you

POCKETS *forcefully grabs her head and tries to shove
her under the covers,* IONA *resists.*

IONA We can – we can do it another time

POCKETS CHRIST ON A / FUCKING POGO STICK can you –

IONA LOOK POCKETS I'M NOT GOIN'

POCKETS You're only sayin' tha' –

IONA I'm not! I'm seriously not!

POCKETS ...Let go – let go of my face stop fuckin' lookin at me –

IONA I want ta stay – you an' me we can –

POCKETS What are ya talkin' about?

Beat.

IONA I don't know how else ta put it Pockets – I'm stayin'! I'm not goin'!

POCKETS Get off – get –

POCKETS pushes IONA off him and gets out of the bed.

He paces the room.

IONA I was only goin' ...cos I'd nothin' here

But I do now

I think you're amazin'

I jus' wanna be around ya

An' I think you wanna be around me

...Dontcha?

Long pause.

POCKETS What about your Dad?

Pause.

Why'd ya make such a song an' dance about goin' so?

IONA I'm allowed change me mind amen't I?

POCKETS Jesus

Jesus

IONA Look the sex thing – it's nothin' ta be embarrassed abou'

POCKETS I'm not embarrassed do I look embarrassed!? – YOU should be embarrassed

IONA Wh-why?

POCKETS Not a clue what you're doin' Jesus no wonder I couldn't – an' now you're stayin' on top of all of this – what did ya think ha we'd go swannin' off inta the sunset, ha? Fuckin' *motts* man

IONA What're ya talkin' abou'?

POCKETS Why're you still in my bedroom?

IONA Just calm down *please*!

POCKETS Made a righ' thick of me haven't ya?

> **POCKETS** *starts gathering up her clothes and throwing them at her.*

IONA Stop it! You said you'd miss me

POCKETS I was just sayin' tha'

IONA You weren't

POCKETS I was

IONA NO YOU WEREN'T YOU WEREN'T YOU DON'T MEAN THA'

Long pause.

Oh my God...

I given up *everythin'* for you

POCKETS I never asked ya ta

...

IONA ...fuck – YOU CAN'T DO THIS TA ME

POCKETS Listen – the *last* thing I want is you stickin' around Iona

Now fuck off

IONA *stands.*

Gets her stuff to go.

Tries not to implode.

Finally manages to gather herself.

She turns and looks him up and down.

IONA You'd wanna get that shit seen to

Ya flaccid *fuck* ya.

Coda:

POCKETS *does a hundred press ups.*

Scene Eleven
Fucked It

Later that day. PINGU's *bedroom.*

PINGU *is in a dull grey T-shirt and not in great form.*

PINGU *unzips their suitcase and slowly starts unpacking.*

They stop and look around. Staring at the walls, or though them, at Crumlin. This place where they're now stuck.

They resume pulling items out of their suitcase.

IONA *enters, unnoticed at first, in a state. She hasn't slept.*

IONA Are ya goin'?

PINGU *rushes to get* IONA *out of the room.*

Hear me out! Please Pingu. I'm so sorry – that's what I came here to say I'm sorry what I did was unforgiveable –

They almost end up in a wrestling match.

I'm stronger than you – I know I'm small but I'm like the fuckin' hulk – look five minutes

PINGU *does not relent...but it's clear* IONA's *going to win.*

I will do anythin' – I'm serious ANYTHIN' PLEASE

PINGU *eventually gets tired and* IONA *wins. They put as much distance between themselves and* IONA *as possible, rubbing their arms where* IONA's *death grip hurts.*

I am, I'm sorry

I can't even believe meself

It really wasn't what it was cracked up ta be

...Pockets...

...

Why does everyone like him so much?

...

...

I'm a total eej, I can't even

PINGU *does not respond. If anything,* **PINGU** *is closer to the* **PINGU** *we see when they shut down to protect themselves around the others – indecipherable.*

Don't do that ta me

Don't do what you do with everyone else

Please – we're best friends Pingu

PINGU *has to snort at that.*

IONA *takes a step towards* **PINGU**. *They flinch.*

Sorry –

Jesus I'd never hurt ya

...

That day you moved in

I seen you by the kerb there in your suit fuckin' directin' the movers in an' out like an airport controller!

An' I thought

Now *that* is someone I can get along with

Hah?

I never questioned it

I never asked ya

I never fuckin' needed ta

...

You mean the world ta me ya do

Me heart's about ta burst here

But **PINGU** *won't concede.*

I'm askin' ya this once

Please, *please* just say somethin'

Just say "I forgive you"

Say whatever you want but please I'm beggin' ya just say somethin' please

Say you love me back

Say we're mates

Say you love me like I love you

Say it!!!!!!!

I'm sorry – I'm sayin' I'm sorry!!!

Nope.

What more d'ya want? Blood!? I said I'm sorry!

PINGU *crosses their arms. Time for* **IONA** *to go.*

Please look we can't throw away everythin' just over – me bein' an arsehole for one minute righ'?

IONA *makes to go to* **PINGU** *again but this time* **PINGU** *makes it clear* **IONA** *is not to come near.*

Oh for fuck's sake – okay look I'm sorry but *you* were the one pushin' me ta move when I wasn't ready – yeah! Ya were! Yet here I am – I'm still up for bein' mates! Your hands aren't clean here either!!!

PINGU *opens the door for* **IONA** *to leave,* **IONA** *instantly slams it.*

I'm jus' sayin' okay!!!! So can we not both just forgive each other an' move on?

You can be angry at me all ya like but if I were you – I'd be angry at *you* – fuck – *I'm* angry at you – okay – it takes two ta tango righ'? These things don't happen ourra nowhere

A shoe flies past **IONA**'s *head.*

Tha fuck!?

More things flying at **IONA** *now –* **PINGU** *is hurling things at her from their suitcase.*

Jesus! What's wrong wit' you!

But **PINGU** *is pelting* **IONA**.

Ow! OW!

Oh right yeh just throw your clothes why dontcha oh very mature VERY MATURE

PINGU *picks up the suitcase to throw,* **IONA** *pegs it out the door.*

Oh fuck that!

PINGU *slams the door, leans against it, and takes a moment.*

Scene Twelve
I See You

The jacks at Matt The Rashers.

TOLLER *is just shutting the toilet door when a foot appears, jamming it. Soon a whole body is forcefully trying to squeeze in as* **TOLLER** *wrestles the door. It is* **PINGU.**

TOLLER Get OFF!!!!!

They struggle. **PINGU** *wins and slips in, locking the door.*

I'm burstin' Pingu –

PINGU *clenches and unclenches their fists – a coiled spring.*

I'm about ta piss down me leg here!

PINGU *turns around to face the door.*

Ah that's not funny!

Me rashers and sausages are sittin' out there gettin' cold JUST LET ME PISS IN PEACE

PINGU *doesn't move.*

I heard about what happened after I left last nigh'

Well I saw it on snapchat

Look if you're here for revenge you're in the wrong place I didn't do anythin'!

PINGU *doesn't budge.*

Look are ya okay?

Seriously are ya okay?

Will ya still go d'ya think?

PINGU *shrugs. Shakes their head. Confused, puts their head in their hands.*

TOLLER *stares at* **PINGU** *a while, not sure what to do. Then makes a decision.*

Ah pet

Ah now c'mere

TOLLER *goes to hug* **PINGU** *but* **PINGU** *flinches as soon as she raises her arms.*

Sorry – sorry

TOLLER *hovers, no idea what to do with* **PINGU**.

So they can be real cunts as you've discovered

Eventually **TOLLER** *sits.*

I'm out in the cold now big time an' all

Went round Kelly Phelan's earlier, she told me ta get fucked, told me she'd been waitin' years ta say tha'

Been starin' at the four walls at home goin' fuckin' mad – that's why I'm so excited for me fuckin' rashers!!!!!

Long pause.

Not nice is ih?

PINGU *looks at her.*

...well...they never been nice ta me

But this is a whole new level

Long pause.

Can I tell you somethin' very lame?

I actually always thought you were alrigh'

I don't care what y'are

If I'm honest Pingu,

I think you're kind of great

PINGU ...

TOLLER One – you've the patience of a saint putting up with Iona all this time – I don't know how ya manage she's like a fuckin' mollusk an' Two – you don't give a fuck what people think of ya

PINGU ...

TOLLER I wish I could be like you

Just...yourself.

PINGU ...

TOLLER Fuck 'em

The lot of them

They don't deserve ya

You deserve ta go Pingu ya know tha'? Somewhere better than here

Christ can I come with ya?

– jokin' –

I'd love ta go ta London

I'd go over there an' I'd get meself ta loads of auditions an' be a dancer in a music video that's what I'd do

Major craic

...

Get some friends that actually like me

...

Ah.

I'd never manage.

Stuck here, amen't I?

...

Not you though, ha?

TOLLER *and* **PINGU** *look at each other.*

A moment of mutual respect, or humanity, or something.

Can I ask ya somethin'?

Will ya fuck off before me bladder explodes?

PINGU *gets up.*

They nod to each other.

PINGU *goes.*

Scene Thirteen
Bros Before Hoes

County Glen Estate. The boys shadowbox.

POCKETS Absolutely *burst* the ring off her so I did

TRIX *jabs.*

Squealin' like a gutted pig she was...

Jab. Jab – cross.

Waddled outta there

TRIX *jabs.*

Absolutely –

TRIX Yeh I get it, ya rode her, d'ya want a bleedin' medal?

POCKETS Alrigh'! Christ!

Sore loser wa'?

TRIX *does an impressive, if slightly overly aggressive combo.*

Ah next time pal, next time

Not without her surprises wa? Motts, hah?

TRIX How'd'ya mean?

POCKETS Ah, ya know –

TRIX Go mad over the videos did she?

POCKETS ...Hah?

TRIX Oh – is that not what you –?

POCKETS Wait – videos?

TRIX Honestly, not a big deal – what were you gonna say?

POCKETS No – what're ya talkin' bout?

TRIX Ah...eh

Ah just a few people been circulatin' some eh footage a the two a you eh...scorin' last nigh' is all

POCKETS ...birra scorin' so what?

TRIX Ah yeh yeh

Just eh

POCKETS What?

TRIX Well eh...they're havin' a bit of a laugh over it

POCKETS ...Why?

TRIX Not exactly Ariana Grande is she?

Yeh they're callin' it the Beast and the Beast

Ya know – like Beauty and the Beast

Except. You're both...

POCKETS You fuckin' serious?

TRIX Bit of eh...speculation as well as ta whether you had a threesome – you, Iona an' Pingu like

POCKETS WHAT? I NEVER TOUCHED PINGU!

TRIX I know! I know! Here I wouldn't worry man I've got your back – told them ta lay off

POCKETS WHO'S GOIN' ROUND SAYIN' THA'?

TRIX Dunno – fewa the lads – I'll find out for ya

Maybe just don't spread it around that ya shagged her ya know?

Beat.

POCKETS You're windin' me up

TRIX I'm not man

POCKETS What videos? There's no videos – this is bullshit

TRIX *gets his phone out and – as he opens Snapchat:*

TRIX Mate she's an absolute rotter, you could see that righ'?
I mean you wouldn't ride her inta battle

POCKETS *watches the video.*

POCKETS An' everyone's laughin' at me?

TRIX I mean she's a face like a bag of hammers Pockets.
An' you smashed that.

Beat.

POCKETS *You* were tryin' ta smash her!

TRIX Was I?

POCKETS Yeah! Ya know you were! You couldn'ta been tryin' harder!?

TRIX Don't remember tha'

POCKETS IT WAS YESTERDAY

TRIX I'd sooner fuck a hungry bear.

POCKETS YOU'D SOONER –!?

TRIX Whatever – look – what I'm sayin' is – No one talks shit about you, not on my watch, know what I'm sayin'? We'll put an end ta this

POCKETS That's fuckin' right!
I'll fuckin' burst them the *cunts*

TRIX Sure look she'll be gone soon annyway everyone'll forget quick enough

POCKETS *hesitates at this.*

What dya thinka me tracksuit?

POCKETS Hah?

TRIX Me gear? Ya like ih? Feelin' fresh so I am

POCKETS How'd ya get tha'?

TRIX Nicked it didn't I? Seriously I wouldn't worry 'bout all tha' – main thing is – you got your leg over an' at the enda the day – who can argue with a birra gee ha?

POCKETS Look I didn't ride her alrigh'?

TRIX Hah?

POCKETS I didn't fuck her!

TRIX Why not?

POCKETS What d'ya mean why not a second ago you were sayin' scarlet for me FOR ridin' her jesus I can't win!

TRIX Alrigh' – cool your jets

POCKETS She's unhinged is why

TRIX Really!?

POCKETS Yeh. Chronic liar.

Went fuckin' nuts at me last nigh' turned out she was lyin' this whole fuckin' time – she was never fuckin' goin'

TRIX NO

POCKETS Serious. Made the whole bleedin' thing up.

TRIX Fuck off

POCKETS Yeh. Just wanted the attention.

TRIX Wow... WOW... That is not cool

POCKETS Honestly you shoulda seen it – beggin' me ta be her boyfriend

She hit the fuckin' roof when I said I'd no interest

TRIX Jesus ya see some stuff on Red Pill bout clingy motts but ya never expect it in real life ya know?

POCKETS Honestly if she'd had handcuffs she'd've shackled herself ta me I'm not messin'

TRIX D'ya know what I'm not fuckin' surprised, there was clearly somethin' wrong wit' her from day one, fuckin' bitch.

So she definitely not goin'?

POCKETS NO – an' now this video craic? Jaysus it's a fuckin' car crash

Gonna be sleepin' with one eye open for the rest of me life now knowin' she still lives round the corner, wa?

Beat. **TRIX** *lowers his paws and contemplates.*

What?

Are ya havin' a fit or somethin', WHAT?

TRIX I'm thinkin'!

TRIX *looks at* **POCKETS,** *he's just had an idea.*

Scene Fourteen
The Last Supper

IONA *is in Texas Chicken eating her misery.*

She is surrounded by greasy debris.

TOLLER *enters.*

IONA Alrigh'?

TOLLER Alrigh'
State of you.

IONA ...I've actually eaten enough ta fill a tank
I might actually be sick
I feel fuckin' awful
You can join me in me pity party if ya like
I've fucked ih, haven't I?
Really fucked ih
What am I gonna do?

TOLLER Fucked if I know

IONA I can't go back ta school next week
Pingu won't so much as look at me
Afraid ta walk down the fuckin' street at this point
(beat) Toller?

TOLLER *What?*

IONA ...Will you be my mate?

TOLLER No pet.

IONA Why? Why not? What is so fuckin' wrong wit' me, hah?
Why can't people see I'm... I'm –

TOLLER Someone did Iona.

...

Why the fuck would you not've gone? Seriously?

This place is a fuckin' tip

People only goin' ta school for the chance to swing at the fuckin' teachers

Can't look left or right but someone's tearin' strips off ya for something you've done or not done or even just thought about doin', jesus it's exhaustin'

IONA *looks at her. You. The answer is you.*

Your only options become a fuckin' taxi driver, a hairdresser or a fuckin' drug dealer

Is that it like?

You could actually've been someone, you know tha'?

Why – I'm serious tell me – why would ya not get out if ya had half the fuckin' chance? Why'd ya sack it in like tha'?

IONA ...I don't know where my Da lives

...I don't even know what he looks like anymore

Long pause.

TOLLER I think they're gonna go ya know

I mean I've no idea cos they don't talk but

I think they are

IONA ...oh fuck

Oh *fuck*

IONA *jumps up, not even sure what she has to do, just knowing she has to do something.*

Scene Fifteen
A Goodbye Of Sorts

Early evening.

Eamon Ceannt Park, Crumlin.

IONA *waits nervously with a backpack and large box.*

She is wearing the minging white Crocs, proudly.

She is in an eclectic mixture of clothes...a huge cardigan – like a beast of a cardigan. A weird spangly dress. Just weird-ass stuff, clearly a collection of her favourite clothes from down the years.

She takes out her phone, does a boomerang, and posts it to her story.

*After a while – so long she fears they may never turn up – **PINGU** appears with their suitcase.*

Loathe to be there, but there nonetheless. They look at their watch.

IONA Howiye

Thanks for comin'

I won't keep ya

...

So I've got a eh

A confession

I own these crocs

They're mine

An' they are comfortable as fuck

An' they are *so* practical

...

Eh this *(the cardigan)* is Mam's. She gave it ta me a few years ago when I was real down about...ya know everythin' goin' on

...

An' this was me party dress when I was in primary... I was always the real fuckin' belle of the ball in this yoke so

So "fuck ih" is what I'm sayin'

She takes a photo and posts it to her stories.

I don't care annymore.

...

But look I don't wanna make this about me – but jus' quickly –

She hands PINGU *a box. It's the Pumas cut to ribbons.*

They weren't worth it

IONA *presents the next box.*

She gestures PINGU *to open it.*

Yeh so... Did some research and this is all stuff you need ta be gettin' around London in one piece

So eh first things first – the tube: I hear the only decent one's the Victoria line – and don't be goin' near the Central line, misery apparently

I also want ta point out – this – what the fuck're they doin' callin' the place

COCKfosters!!!????

Anyway.

Eh...some Taytos – course – an' a chicken fillet roll – they don't have them over there cos they're savages

I got ya this eh tape roller thing for your suit – can't be goin' out with fluff all over ya

PINGU *looks through the box.*

A few other things – I know the Queen an' Meghan Markle an' tha' might seem excitin' but I want you to remember: that aul bitch an' her people oppressed us for 800 years alrigh'? So don't go pallyin' up ta them. I've packed ya a tricolour so ya don't forget where you're from.

IONA *pulls out the Tricolour and wraps it around* PINGU's *shoulders.*

Okay it's not great cos I'm no artist but...

I made ya this

It's a passport. It's not legal tender but –

She hands it to PINGU. PINGU *thumbs it. It's a hand drawn, makeshift passport.*

You'll have ta use your real one ta board the plane an' tha'

But this one says eh

This one says who you really are –

PINGU *leafs through the passport. They slip it into a pocket.*

Thank you.

An' I just want ta say

Actually hold on –

She gets her phone out again.

PINGU *tries to get her to put it away.*

No – no seriously I want everyone ta hear this

Pingu ya shouldn't have ta go

There should be a place for ya here

But there's not

An' that's not righ'

But you are gonna smash ih, alrigh'?

I'm prouda ya

She puts the phone away.

I am.

Beat.

An' sure look if ya do change your mind I've me bag all packed, I can run home an' get it quickly – I've nicked me Mam's credit card, so we could go over there an' smash it – I was thinkin' you know what I should be? A radio host! I can talk for Ireland – might as well get paid for it ya know? Get us into all the big festivals – everyone here'll be so fuckin' jealous, honestly I'd kill ta see the look on Trix and Pockets' faces when they see we're such big deals. What d'ya think? You've my ticket booked dontcha?

PINGU *doesn't move.*

Well just eh – do the online check-in there

Beat.

Pingu – do the online check in an' I can come!

TOLLER *runs in out of breath.*

TOLLER Lads what're you doin' here? You need ta go

IONA I'm just sayin' goodbye!

TOLLER I'm serious – Trix an' Pockets they've seen your Stories

IONA Good!

TOLLER Not fuckin' good! They're on their way – Trix is live streamin' it

IONA Toller babes I've got this

TOLLER No you've not! Look just – go! Go get your flight gwan!

The boys arrive, **TRIX** *already with his phone out.*

TRIX Alrigh'? What's this?

TOLLER *(to* **IONA** *and* **PINGU***)* I'm serious!

TRIX You alrigh' Pingu?

POCKETS Surprised ta see ya with Iona here

TRIX After what she did to you?

POCKETS Yeh sure if I was you I'd be ragin'

IONA You just seen on me stories I've said sorry!

TRIX Houndin' ya puttin' her apology online I mean come on

IONA What? I was –

TRIX What she gives you a few niknaks and everything's forgotten? Yeh righ'

POCKETS Hardly an apology is it?

IONA That's not –

TRIX I'd be fuckin' volcanic so I would mate

POCKETS Hittin the fuckin' roof I would be

IONA Stop it! I AM sorry!

TOLLER Fuck sake Pingu just go!

TRIX You shouldn't be the one havin' ta go. Why don't ya send *her* packin'?

POCKETS Teach her a lesson even

TOLLER Christ – *lads* –

TRIX I mean – was she ever even your friend?

IONA You two're fuckin' scum ya know tha'?

I can't believe I ever wanted ta be mates wit' you lot – ya get that in your little video?

POCKETS Who d'ya think you're talkin' to?

TRIX Remember how you were a fuckin' nobody til we came along?

IONA Yeh. Bliss it was.

Anyway. Glad ya came – I knew you'd be round like flies on dogshit when ya saw me stories.

Pingu – I've one final leaving gift for you:

IONA *goes to her backpack and pulls out a hamster ball, with Benny inside.*

POCKETS No

TRIX What the fuck is that?

POCKETS NO – HOW'D YOU GET THA'?

IONA Everyone – this is Benny

TRIX BENNY!?

IONA Pockets' beloved hamster

POCKETS It's not mine

TRIX Benny!!!! AH-HA

POCKETS I don't know where she got tha'

IONA *(to* PINGU*)* I made the wrong choice before

    I should've chosen you

    But I'm choosin' you now

She gets her phone out and again, feeds live to Insta –.

Pockets fuckin' loves this here hamster, it's his big fuckin' secret

TRIX AH-HAHAHAHAAAAAAAAAAAA

POCKETS Shurrup

TRIX *gets his camera out once more to film, but* POCKETS *wallops it out of his hand.*

TOLLER Pockets where'dya get that?

TRIX AAAHAHAHAHAHAHAHAHAHA

POCKETS SHUTTHAFUCKUP

TRIX Jesus I always knew you were a fuckin' pussy but this is somethin' else – BENNY!? KINDA NAME IS THA'!? SOUNDS LIKE A GEOGRAPHY TEACHER

IONA See Pingu? See what I'd do for you?

(to POCKETS) Big man aren't ya?

POCKETS Fuck you

IONA This isn't the only little secret I'm sittin' on

POCKETS You *fuckin'* dare –

TOLLER Hold on – was that Paddy's hamster?

TRIX BEN-NY! BEN-NY! BEN-NY! (Etc)

TOLLER Conor? Did he leave it t'ya?

(beat. Emotional) Oh my God

TRIX *is roaring. He's managed to grab his phone again and he's recording.*

TRIX I'm sorry but if them videos of you an' Iona weren't enough – this is the cherry on the fuckin' cake

POCKETS STOP FILMIN' GIMME DA

IONA ...What videos?

TRIX The two a' you scorin'

IONA What d'ya mean?

TRIX Everyone is DYIN' over these

TRIX *gets the videos up and plays them to* IONA *who watches aghast.*

IONA ...why?

TRIX Cos you're rank Iona, why d'ya think!?

Christ let me get a photo of you in that get up an' all, the fuckin' hack of ya

TOLLER Trix stop it that's enough

TRIX This is gold

TOLLER I'm serious Trix – stop ih jus' stop bein' a cunt *for once*!

POCKETS Iona – Benny.

IONA Do you think I'm rank?

Do ya!?

Have you been laughin' at me an' all?

Beat.

I know you feel somethin' for me – I KNOW ya do

TRIX Eh Pockets...do you wanna tell her? Or shall I?

IONA What!? Tell me what?!

...Pockets.

TRIX Well. We were only tryin' ta see who could get their leg over before ya fucked off ta London

Kinda ruined it with the whole 'not goin' thing didn'tja?

And bein' frigid...

And your terrible face...

IONA *is dumbstruck.* **TRIX** *comes right in to get a close up with his camera.*

IONA *(to* **POCKETS***)* That true?

POCKETS *stares at the floor.*

IONA *puts Benny in his ball on the ground.*

She stamps and stamps and stamps.

POCKETS FUCK JESUS

TRIX Holy...

TOLLER IONA STOP! JESUS CHRIST!

She finishes.

She collects herself.

POCKETS Fuckin' mental bitch

Yeh. You are.

You are fuckin' rank.

POCKETS *goes to leave.*

Toller?

Pause.

TOLLER No.

POCKETS *turns to go.*

POCKETS Don't follow me.

TRIX Ah lighten up –

POCKETS I mean ih.

Don't come round anymore.

POCKETS *goes.*

TRIX *digests this...*

Then rights himself.

TRIX *(on his phone)* Honestly this is some top quality content lads. Benny is now a pancake.

IONA *starts to cry.*

It gets louder and louder.

Stop that will ya?

Iona stop ih

Stop it!

Slowly, **TRIX** *puts the phone down.*

Take a joke wouldja?

It's not that bad

IONA *wails.*

Christ

...

Look sorry alrigh'?

...

Fuck.

He goes.

TOLLER *(to* PINGU*)* Would ya ever take me with ya?

PINGU *takes a deep breath, turns to* TOLLER, *and shakes their head 'No'.*

...Good luck.

Beat. TOLLER *goes.*

IONA Please

Please please please...

PINGU *packs up the box and hands it back to* IONA.

Please...

PINGU *shakes their head and turns to go.*

I stood up for you.

PINGU *stops.*

For years and years and years and years I stood up for you

An' it was *tirin'* Pingu

Snappin' back at every insult, every bad word, *every time* someone even looked at ya funny. I fucked up ONCE and I put my hands up on tha' – I did – I was a cunt – but I was THERE – when you got beat up – when you got cans'a coke poured down your suit – when you couldn't get out

of bed – I was fuckin' there every single fuckin' time. An' I
never asked for anything back. I never fuckin' did.

PINGU ...

IONA I know I'm not a good person I know tha' but *you* need
ta know you're just as fuckin' bad

Pingu so get off your high fuckin' horse alrigh'?

You've no fuckin' heart Pingu you know tha'? No fuckin'
heart – cos if you did –

PINGU *goes to speak.*

Then – you know what?

Decides against it.

She's not worth it.

Oh that's righ' – yeh – that's righ' don't say a fuckin' word
as usual

I'm just not worth breakin' your vow of silence for – hardly
important enough am I?

PINGU ...

IONA You're gonna fail – ya know tha'? That's a fact. You'll be
crawling back to me sure enough – give it three weeks. I'd
put money on ih.

That's all I wanted ta say, you can fuck off now.

PINGU *leaves, heartbroken but head held high.*

I am gonna be such a big fuckin' deal Pingu

You've no idea!!!

You'll be readin' about me in the fuckin' paper you will

I'm gonna be somebody

Me

Me!

Not you

Me.

...

Me.

PROPS/LIGHTNING/SOUND EFFECTS

It's probably best not to use a real hamster for Benny.

It's up to you to find a creative solution for the frequent shifts in location and time.

Music should reflect contemporary music young people are listening to.

VISIT THE SAMUEL FRENCH BOOKSHOP AT THE ROYAL COURT THEATRE

Browse plays and theatre books, get expert advice and enjoy a coffee

Samuel French Bookshop
Royal Court Theatre
Sloane Square
London
SW1W 8AS
020 7565 5024

Shop from thousands of titles on our website

 samuelfrench.co.uk

 samuelfrenchltd

 samuel french uk

Lightning Source UK Ltd.
Milton Keynes UK
UKHW021834011019
350811UK00006B/73/P